The Unspoken Heart

SPICEE GRAY

Purposely Created
PUBLISHING GROUP

The Unspoken Heart

Copyright © 2014 Spicee Gray

Published by Purposely Created Publishing Group™

Printed in the United States of America

ISBN: 0-615-99099-1
ISBN-13: 978-0-615-99099-6

For more information, log onto
www.PurposelyCreatedPG.com

Dedication

The Unspoken Heart is dedicated out of love for my beautiful dear mother, Mrs. Kathryn A. Huff aka Mrs. K. Huff—the one woman that is not only the other part of my heart, but my inspiration through every struggle, having constructed me into the woman and mother that I am today.

The wings of my mother are always covered in prayer, or by the strong words of wisdom which guided me to stand on my feet through the many storms and scars in my life.

Her footprints in my life have enabled me to fight and brush off the dust from my knees, for trouble don't last always and joy comes in the morning.

She has been the sweet melody of the morning rise and the tenderness of comfort in the moonlight rest.

She is the mother of devotion.

She is the woman of dedication.

She is the friend of understanding.

She is the birth of unconditional love.

She is a God's gift of life.

In my eyes, my mother is and always will be the beat of my heart.

Table of Contents

Sentiments from The Heart

Acknowledgments

I've always known that I would write a book. It couldn't be just any old book, however. It was imperative that I wrote one that pertained to all of life's struggles that had been buried in the depths of my heart. That being said, I would like to take this time to give thanks to God, my Father, for everything I've accomplished and the woman I have become in order to possess the one key to healing and escape. I would have never known the scars within me could turn into words that people would be touched by and, in turn, inspire to put forth what I have within these pages.

Thanks to all my Facebook friends, my co-workers, childhood friends, and the many others that I've met over the years. Special thanks to my mother who pushed me to expand my gift of poetry for not just for publishing purposes, but to help reach out to others that have been through similar life trials as myself or worse. Most of all, thank you to the ones who have scarred and hurt me emotionally, physically and verbally. If it had not been for you, this poetry would not be. For not only is it a melody to my heart, but it's also healing for the lost ones.

The photos of Ms. Spicee contained within *The Unspoken Heart* is with great appreciation and love for Marvelous Creation by Mr. Stephan Pendarvis.

Stephan is more than a mere man of photography. He captures beauty in motion with the gifted eye of creation from God. He has been a tremendous inspiration, encouragement, and light in my walk towards formatting this melody of poetry.

I can truly say with sincerity and confidence that he has helped me focus on what God has instilled in me in order to be an inspiration to others—through not just my story, but also in my writing. Stephan is one of many that God has placed in my life—not for a season, but a reason and I embrace those gifts that have maintained availability through my storms. Thank you Stephan, and may God bless you as He has continuously done for me.

I would also love to show great appreciation to an extraordinary woman who not only escaped from bondage, but was able to stand her own ground and look to her children who'd issued her strength. Ms. Imelda Recio is the reason that the title of this book exists. She'd chimed in on Facebook, suggesting that *The Unspoken Heart* should be the name of this book "for all that you write is from your heart." I am ever so grateful to my Heavenly Father for placing such a beautiful woman in my life who has inspired me to see what has been instilled within my heart, which is the ability to help others through my melody of writing. She is one of many who inspired me to never give up on a dream that directs not only my life, but others towards a road of healing. Thank you, Imelda Recio and may God bless you as your path continues to form riches within your own life.

To Mr. Charles Dobard, thank you for being a good friend and mentor! You showed me how I deserved to be treated—as a queen, protected, and nourished with love. You are the reason *The Unspoken Heart* was born and formed as a door of healing to help others that had been abused or suffering from domestic violence. You are a good man, and I will forever cherish you for helping me realize that I am a beautiful woman and worthy of true happiness.

Introduction

Every woman desires nothing more than to be understood, and we all, meaning every single one of us, deserve to be treated with respect. When a man takes a woman as his wife, there is a spiritual requirement that both, husband and wife, are obligated to fulfill.

The fifth chapter of Ephesians, verse 25, states that husbands should love their wives just as Christ loved the church and gave Himself for it. Likewise, just as Christ is head of the church, husbands were divinely designed to be head of the household.

Though he is the head, he is expected to stand next to her, dwelling within his presiding position; furthermore, he demonstrates his love for his wife by prioritizing her needs in understanding and by honoring her as the weaker vessel.

Mother's Heartfelt Words

I mentioned him to my child for quite some time. I was impressed by him from the short moment of being in his presence.

To my child I stressed that the meaning of "I love you" is singular, defining that it's you and no one but you.

If you have been abused, he will be there standing, assisting one in aide of healing, understanding the extent of your heart's fear.

He would be willing to wait for you and you only in order to display that he is not as those who hurt you or sliced your heart.

To represent himself as a man of God, realizing that woman is the weakest vessel would make his presence known in manner to repair you. Not taking her for granted just to think of himself as well as his own flesh.

Considering all his actions to be Christ-like, or should he be questioning himself?

Does he have the true love as Christ when He gave His only son?

Should he be questioning himself if it is of meaning that she fell in love with him and cries in pain?

Did he honestly give her the choice to wait in line, or does he truly know what love is?

Out of the multitude of women in this world, does he want them all?

Or does he want the one he left in tears?

Did he ever question if he had unintentionally taken her heart for granted not realizing to handle with care?

Nevertheless, if he states he loves her, but he is not embracing one in commitment for his feelings appear to be as loving everyone.

I told her to open the heart, for it was time to heal and allow him to love her with all the goodness I foreseen in him to make her happy.

To hear my child once again in heartfelt tears surfaced all thoughts of regret within the words of: "Mom, I really do love him!" It was a shock, because I knew my child refused entrance of any man or any acceptance of love.

Mrs. K. Huff

Once abused, "[s]he now sits represented, graciously refusing one to change the hands of time."

— Spicee Gray

The Hardened Heart

ରରର

Heart miles became weary of trials,
throbbing in open sore,

Patience has eventually expired throughout
the dreary years,

My eyes completely drained dry behind one's tears,

Bold loneliness has stood still constantly
knocking at my door,

Quietly awaiting change one realized
she refuse doing it anymore,

Countless chances has hurdled out on
what you refuse to clearly see,

Look closely within and acknowledge
what one has afflicted upon me,

My weakening heart has slowly hardened
towards becoming totally warned,

The muscles in coordination with her soul
have completely been scorned,

God witnessed towards clear blue sight hindermost
all you have put me through,

So the deepening applied inflicted wounds my friend
is all solemnly on you,

Be mindful of the heartless flowing words through parted
lips that one shall say,

For letters applied in moments clicking calculation will
equal out towards double pay,

He lacks acknowledgement towards pain that dwells
within depths of my heart,

Slowly resulting in cause for my love inward deep to be
torn completely apart,

One merely refused issuance of respect as I had
devotionally supplied to you,

So my love for him eventually diminished and validated
to be totally through,

Contemplating if you had sacrificed all desiring,
truly wanting to be with me,

Deciding my value in shedding one more tear and
demanding finally setting all free,

So I slowly closed the lids, blocking out one radiant
stream for glaring peeping light,

Visualizing pulling you closely—breathing, wrapping and
one holding me extremely tight,

Elevation of the heat rise as our lips start to momentarily
gently and instantly touch,

Speed per hour one's heart races in time towards minute
hand becoming no matter of such,

As the shades cover to sighted vision drifts state as each
one began to eventually open up,

Drunkard emotions swiftly pour smoothly, rising above
heightened thin glassed rimmed cup,

Mirrored reflections in the formed optical sight clearly
translated appearance of me,

Drawn feelings from my strongest muscle sustained
battles flight letting things just to be,

Acceptance that sometimes being alone is healthier than
having someone's loneliness range,

Love never costs one single dollar towards
acknowledgment of a hardened heart's change.

Elimination

ରରର

$\mathcal{L}$ook deep inside my eyes and what do you see?

A story unspoken that has set my soul totally free,

Swords of false tongue can't even tear me down,

For it's a smile on my face you see, not a frown;

The battle was hard for my heart to even endure,

With God's hands covering me, I am protected for sure,

Through every scar that my knees have timely healed,

Are documented reasons my strength is solemnly sealed,

Choices made in order to make my life entirely complete,

Was by standing, quietly observing and hitting delete,

Trusting in mortal man one realized I was falsely led,

In my darkening path I have chosen to turn my head,

As a mother to my children open arms invitingly I spread,

Ones of betrayal in hand, I, without hesitation,
cut the thread,

For in my heart you slowly lost to all
defamation and deceit,

In me through all trials and tribulations you get no receipt,

So in the midst becoming all that one
sincerely wholeheartedly said,

I will end this by saying my prayers and breaking
loaves of bread.

Not For Sale

୧୧୧

Gently I turn my head with thoughts in mind,

Searching for answers to questions of any kind,

I stand strong no matter how the devil tries
to tear me down,

With God's loving hands of protection
you won't see me frown;

Believe what you want, my heart speaks loud and clear,

From within, I sustain any form of fear,

My place I stand alone to take control,

Mind and body, you will never have my soul;

Woman I am and Woman I will be,

No tricks or lies will defeat this one; can't you see?

So speak with false tongue or pull your game,

The ending results will remain the same,

I might shed a tear for a minute or two,

Never will I consider giving in unto you,

So if you're ready, put on your armor of gold,

Cause the fight in my spirit can't be sold!

The Presence

ଋଋଋ

One bench sat for my tiring body to park,

Slowly lowering head for mind to rest,

Stretching legs forward placing feet to nest,

Wind swiftly touching the face with comforting ease,

Mother Nature, don't stop; I'm begging you please,

The night is lingering on as ducks silently sound,

Water beating waves of music oh so loud,

Temperature rising as presence felt known,

A voice interrupts with deepening tone,

Speaking to make me feel safe of normal pace,

Sweet love don't move, stay in your place,

Heat begins rising, making the heart tremble speed,

Don't fret my fragile one; I'm all that you need,

Leaning forward to place on forehead a gentle kiss,

If anything tenderness just remember this,

There's nothing in life that you can't bear,

Hold your head up high cause I'm always there,

I open my eyes with feet flat on land,

No one was there but His footprints in the sand.

Give Thanks

ରେରେରେ

As you experience many of life's changes,

Trials and tribulation comes in different ranges,

Through each test, learn how growth brings strength,

No matter tensions width or even its length;

Time moves in more than one motion,

Look to our children and submit the devotion,

For in life, chances you are granted just one,

The battle is the Lord's, not yours to be won;

He sees and hears all your fallen tears,

Embraces and protects you from all your fears,

Take your energy and place it in His hands to hold,

You're His child that He carefully formed to mold,

If anything, take a stand to your ground,

For in the end, His love can always be found;

He is our Father and a devoted friend,

His commitment will never lead to an end,

He sacrificed His life, so that we may live,

Out of your day to Him what do you give?

In all He asks is just the word you spread,

And to read daily the nutrition of His bread,

Is that too much to even ask of you?

Taking consideration what He sacrificed too,

Now before laying rest in comforting bed,

Don't forget to give thanks to who kept you fed.

A Woman's Worth

ଯେ ଯେ ଯେ

A woman is more valuable than any token,

Her heart is more tender than any word spoken,

Look into her eyes, you will clearly see her love,

She is gentle with peace from purity of a dove,

To raise your hand applying her harm,

Erases all drawn from your former charm,

To say you're sorry doesn't delete the scars,

You took her from cloud nine into seeing stars,

The day will come whether departure or death:

She will be gone and it will take your breath,

To have gained control instills the fear,

Trust reaping what you sow is oh so near;

Take her by the hand, treat her like gold,

For her love is what you carefully mold,

Sustain your anger; walk with all you can,

Being abusive in any form don't make you a man!

Timely Man

୧୧୧

All love and devotion had felt to be in vain,

Weakening eyes overtaken with fear,

No hope for true happiness afar or near,

Gentle comforting arms embrace placing in zone,

Did she want him to stay or just leave her alone?

His voice so deepening that it filled each empty part,

Love was hitting hard bull's eye from one single dart,

Trembling tone expressed, "Let me love you with all I can!"

Is this is a mirage or a real good man?

Inhaling two ways deep, then the emotions just fell:

Is this real? Slow motion time will tell.

The Safe Haste Place
ଶ ଶ ଶ

I lay numb, tears falling to pillow, thinking of you,

Meditating on your smile and wondering without a clue;

Each day never went without feeling your touch,

Knowing how our love inside meant so much,

Your words of tenderness is of sweet music to my ear,

Taking for granted you always soothe my deepening fear,

To bury my head so far into your chest,

So why am I here alone, feeling something is missing?

When we should be lying here passionately kissing,

Realizing sleeping is my only safe place,

It's the only time I can truly see your face.

Falling Walls

ଉଉଉ

Gently lowering her chest flat to bed,

Her mind wonders where this moment to be led,

Slowly turning her head upon the arms positioned to rest,

Closing each eye in darkness the heart put to test,

Heaviness of his hands glide smoothly
up and down the skin,

Relaxing every muscle as she breathes out then deeply in,

He leans forward placing a kiss that raises her emotion,

In mind she questions if this is the man of true devotion?

Turning her, overlooking with eyes of all he admires,

Burning with fear this may be the one man of her desire,

Not only has he taken her to elevated places,

She exhaled the moment a woman
appreciates and embraces,

For all inside she wants is cherish and love,

In him to bring happiness with peace like a purifying dove,

Willing to see where he leads her in what she never had,

A true man who brings joy to heart and takes away scars
that drove her mad.

No Charge

ଓଓଓ

I sit quietly and gently close my eyes,

Thinking of how vigorously time really flies,

Remembering them once sitting on my lap,

Then watching them take their first step
and joyfully I clap;

The things each one of them do just warms my heart,

Knowing their love for me will pierce like a dart,

Not taking for granted my kids are my joys,

Thanking God for my gorgeous girl and handsome boys,

Each day as I think of my three little hearts,

Praying to God until their grown, my presence never parts,

Personality instilled in each one of them,

Fills my heart and the soul become overwhelmed,

They are my strength throughout one's life,

No matter the struggles of longing strife,

One with calmness to fight in his many storms,

The other stands strong of her boldness
in numerous forms,

While the last has his steps to portray no fear of one's talk,

Short in height as he demands attention with his walk,

A mother can't ask for nothing more than
refundable respect,

While in her stand their needs were never in
paths of neglect,

So if anything, remember this in life when
you become large,

For sacrifice with dedication of my love dear children
there's no charge.

A Woman Scorned

When a woman has been scorned,
be careful of words you say,

Handle with care not misleading road signs
in a wrong way,

As she opens heart, accepting all with you in,

Walls are crumbling with time and the head start to spin;

Your heart might speak of what you want at that time,

Realize her surroundings before backing out
at the drop of a dime,

Closing her down to withdraw to love once again in life,

All inside feels torn as if being cut with
a jagged edge knife;

Now she sees the hour glass's sand run inches deep,

For her heart bleeds tears as the wounded child's weep.

Wrong Pastures

ଶ୍ର ଶ୍ର ଶ୍ର

As I slowly lift my head to mirror, what do I see?

Is this form a woman, or is it just me?

Looking deep inside each eye, nothing becomes clear,

All is apparent to emptiness no fulfillment is near,

She spread her arms to all visuals within clear sight,

Everything in her is exhausted from the fight,

Lips she part and speak softly to her heart,

I gave it my all to still feel entirely torn apart,

All she possess passersby spoke into her life,

But not one was willing to deliver her from her strife,

Sadly she wondered if there is just but one,

To bring her news the battle has been won,

Turning the head towards wide open door,

Innocent one spoke, "Mommy, stop crying.
Please, no more!"

Briskly steps boldly being taken by hand,

Loudly speaking, "You're looking in the wrong land!"

Open your eyes before your time is completely up,

Allow your heart to love and let him fill your cup,

You have sacrificed all and in us your energy burn,

But mommy love waits; it's finally your turn.

The Escape

୧୧୧

Standing still as down fall the rain,

Disguising outside visible with pain,

Unveiled face withdrawn from fallen tears,

Cloudy waters hiding all apparent fears,

It's just little things deep inside of me,

Dreaming of what the mind begins to see,

There's nothing in this world I'd rather do,

Than allow thunderstorms to erase outlined images of you.

Slowly lowering eyes to wetness beneath my feet,

Gazes of reflection to focused expression meet,

Wondering how she escaped from instilled scars,

Sleeping soundly in the comfort of unmarked cars,

While raising her head to stars above,

Softly speaking, "Lord, send me peace significant
to a pure white dove."

All as a woman, my heart won't let it be,

In life with strength I need to be set free!

Contemplating

999

$\mathcal{I}$ sit leaning with head resting back,

Mind of tension I decide to completely pack,

Slowly closing eyes, vision appear slightly clear;

Heart beating deeply just wanting you near,

Thirsting the comfort of your warming touch,

Can't you see I'm missing you too much?

Regretting the walls forbidding optical in sight,

You're not just a friend, but a will to fight;

Words expressed years have taken in vain,

Scars and anger had driven me insane,

Taking deep breaths, my heart can finally see,

All designed of you I need and want in me.

Consumption

ଵଵଵ

$\mathcal{W}$hat are these dreams that are consuming me?

Wall has fallen, so why reflections won't let it be?

Eyes are open to what has been struggling token,

All of me realizes what was traumatically broken;

A smile has turn to a painful frown,

The past caused all in me to drown,

I questioned what was wrong with who I am,

Focusing on kids and strictly working for Uncle Sam;

They say you're strong and have it all,

If that was so, why I feel to stumble and fall?

Words continue to run through my head,

Take my hand and allow yourself to be led,

While in my sleep the vision do appear,

Appreciating a man of you being oh so near;

Placing a smile, making me what I become,

Excelling a loving one's moment to come,

So each day I awake to the morning sun above,

Your face is envisioned in heart as my true love.

The Key

ଶ୍ରୀଶ୍ରୀ

Walking swiftly down the unstable road,

Heart weary and tired from the carried load,

Every mark placed has hardened her emotions,

For granted they had taken all her devotions,

The smile camouflages what eyes show in pain,

Feeling all she poured as a woman was in vain;

Within her hand, she possesses the key,

Waiting for lighted path, opening her to see,

There is one with sincerity of that he shares,

Acknowledging extent of hearted pain she can't bear;

Carefully taking her hand with understanding
of wounded heart,

Willing to give guidance, forbidding anything
tearing her apart,

As he draws her near, pulling head towards chest,

Consoling her in heart, putting all to rest,

For he has come, destroying unbreakable walls,

Preventing the feet from stumbles and falls;

She looks up in his gaze with fear once again to love,

Smiling with vocal, "Baby girl,
I'm a godsend peaceful dove."

"Let me love you so you can clearly see,"

"I am the lock that will set your heart free."

In Love by Yourself

୧୧୧

Gently laying hands upon her chest,

Thoughts of deception hinders peaceful rest,

Looking in mirror is reflection of pain,

Tears falling like the showering rain,

Her mind questioned, "Why give him my heart?"

To once again be torn all apart,

Past scars has scorned her inward glow,

Hopes of happiness towards wind do blow,

For once, she able herself to open up,

Acceptance of his comfort and filling her cup,

Pulling her close, making feelings of safe embraces,

Gazing into his eyes, she sees no empty spaces;

He leaves without warning like a thief into night,

Contemplating of his true worth towards the fight,

Portrayed like the seasoning placed on a shelf,

Eyes opened, realizing she was in love all by herself.

Fallen Tears

ㅁㅁㅁ

*A*s she lifts her hands to cover her face,

His echoing words flow slow in pace,

Sharpening pains to heart shift stabbing points,

Numbing vibes raced throughout her joints;

All around seem as thinning air to fade,

Eyes filled with water in blinding shade,

Disbelief this was happening as clear déjà vu,

Assuming all was good between me and you;

Walls are built to protect at comfort zone,

Kept her from feeling deception and being left alone,

She allowed the guards to pull completely down;

His intentions turned her smile to a frown,

Knowing all scars that dwelled inside of me,

How could he be naïve or even see?

All that was in him, I hungered for,

My love and desire just can't bear no more;

The man who I felt would erase all deep fears,

Lying pillow placed my heartfelt tears.

The Vow

ଏଏଏ

As I sit with head bowed to land,

Through my fingers falls the silky sand,

Eyes paused lifeless without a moment's blink,

Putting mind at halts time to patiently think,

What seed did I sow in my life causing reap?

Leaving heart's hour passing so deep,

To be loved, cherished, and protected from all harms,

Drawn closely buried deep within his arms,

On bending knee, gently placing tender kisses—

These are images a woman sincerely misses,

But in her devotion what was to gain?

Just be inflicted from years of pain,

Vowing never again in giving her heart away,

Allowing him entrance then going astray,

While laying back, yielding nature her needs to tend,

Whispering winds exhale her towards sunset end.

A Mother's Rib

❧❧❧

Woman I am that's my stand in loyalty,

Heart high value is worth truth for royalty,

Mind measures kilograms scaling years of pain,

Whence forth morals to love investment was all in vain,

Legs leaping hurdles overcome total obstacles held inside,

Broken promises of security in darkness shadow
he never abide,

Water falls aligned midnight hour
while emotions gradually pour;

Fist in hand on drum she vowed to sustain
wounds no more,

Without a bit of fear her voice rumbled,
dividing pillows in sky,

Thinking wasted devoted time to be loved just flew her by,

Downward pulling skirt train resembling of her eyes trace,

Tender innocence for one who wrapped arms
around legs in embrace,

Awakening her innocence glowing face
she simply just missed;

Little girl she birthed, the forehead she gently
laid a sweet kiss,

Two matured women with daughter no longer in her crib,

Uniting forces relating as best friends
formed each other's rib,

Heart they share can't divide the waters in a pond,

Mother and daughter's love is of legal oaths bond.

Dwelling Fear

ରରର

Standing in boldness her arms she folds,

Heartaches and scars transformed a mold,

Through years of pain one's mind built the wall,

Refusing entrance of deception at any man's call,

Denying needs toward bonding embracement touch,

Barriers shielded emotions entrance far too much;

Appearance in piercing eyes his heart she desire,

Character of possession captured all her vision admire,

Walking tall with arrogance to draw women in,

Inhaling deep breaths, slowly counting to ten;

Hazel eyes show depth towards true male sincerity,

All deserved as a woman he instilled with clarity,

Acknowledging walls consisting of
a mere mirage hiding ground,

Feared past trauma in him traces could not be found

Touching soul he brought out love in her broken heart,

Still she fear dwelling place in him will be torn apart,

Taking each day while it swiftly just past,

Embracing moments with him while time morally lasts;

How the future ends up only God truly knows,

Adhering to standards as particular cool wind blows.

Bought Out Within

ꠦꠦꠦ

*A*llocating rigorous body abruptly on the bed,

Pondering in aid desiring her soul to be fed,

Keepsake thoughts attributing first visuals of you,

Distinctive moral qualities is like sweet morning dew,

Continually dwelling in the midst of my utmost needs,

In you I found strength where no man had planted seeds,

Pulling me uphill standing presence resembling a dream,

Heavy hands massage muscles parted lips
surrender my scream,

Her arms opened wide apparently seeing the true destiny,

Love and foundation had determined his inspiration in me,

He holds the key of obligation to unlock any closed door,

Within him I found whatever quantity
throughout any store,

Cognizant inside, he whole heartedly is the one,

Time alone with this man brings joy under her sun.

Broken Barriers

ඬඬඬ

Focus towards heart's melody consumed in me,

Transparent message held eyes captive to clearly see,

Hardness of walls formed a dark lonely hiding place,

Woman altered from child dressed in handcrafted lace,

Understand my strength's existence that visually
abides inches deep;

Sweet low song of scars yield painful souls
to passionately weep,

Declaring termination of generational female revile,

Sing the sonata from within love extended in denial,

Breaking all barriers acknowledging
my honest worth's merit,

Awaiting her desiring acceptance of devotional
diamond's carat.

Sweet Endearment

ଉଉଉ

Walking in stride presenting a bouquet of flowers,

Taking only on his mind wonders towards high towers,

The words are endearing lyrics to her preferred song,

Dancing in his arms strenuous chills transmitted long,

Fullness of lips softly exert rounded head to meet,

While he lowers hand in water slowly pouring on feet,

Daydreaming as stars leave footprints across the sky,

Realizing sometimes you don't need a plane to even fly,

Taking her by the hand he lays body on green fields,

Making love toward interposing heart's
instilment from yields,

Acknowledging I've been loved from a man's
indifference range,

Satisfying my soul with sweet distinctive
endearment's change,

He has taken her to never before visual lined traces,

The one true man abiding in heart she firmly embraces.

More than a Woman

இஇஇ

*P*ouring entire life into loving a single member
of the human race,

Satisfying pleasures consisting of his needs as she soberly
moves in pace,

Intentions of tearing down all possessed within her
confining character's mold:

His deep, inheriting, corruptive words causes her emotions
to rapidly fold,

Stepping out enemies lines grasping authority for
deserving constituting heart,

Denying granting entrance towards capacities destructive
intentions torn apart;

Inappreciative for qualities he concluded to visually
discover from afar,

Amounting nights alone had him pleading strong
inclination on a star;

Expiration in uninterrupted succession
filled him with compromising sorrow,

Rejecting acceptance foreseeing the sunrise of
emptiness towards tomorrow,

Collecting in keepsake all one imprints he distressed
treating as a token,

For she is more than a woman, her strength and stance
sits well-spoken.

Behind Solitary Hiding Walls

ଯ ଯ ଯ

She pressed her back firmly to the upright
structured stone,

Emotions shielded one's heart destitute
empowering being left alone,

Shadow's past lurked her every awakening dimming light,

Recollection of feared episodic halting secession
motive to fight;

Consciousness aided towards presence representing
armored oppositional distress,

Peering from around converging lines she begins accepting
becoming his mistress,

Attention breaks obstruction at a distance
receptacle hands call,

Rescuing statistic from behind her years of solitary
hiding wall,

Vision cleared of darkness fading all that abide,

He depicted as a written real property given in stride,

Stilled fear lurks her every motioned steps
consisting doubt,

The unveiling in his former response diminishes
instead of sprouts.

The Modified Transgressing Interchange

ଵ ଵ ଵ

Standing in reflective glass mere image she gaze,

Endurance of disreputable injurious effect
evolve distressing maze,

Everything bounded harbor depths in solitude fiery rage,

Comprehending her inward strength as she
reverses forty in age;

Vision through transparent glass revel
towards beauteous heart,

Woman of resentment transformed darkness into light,

Modified transgressing interchange validate
imprinted sight,

Wisdom processed through conscientiousness
renewed brightening glow;

She raised her arms, smiling and flipping hair
as winds vigorously blow,

Notwithstanding anyone to enter one's gates
or break solid ground;

I am loving being of phenomenal inspiration
to presence all around,

The female dwelling and seen accept her
as she has developed to be,

For what's given from heart is truly consisted
entirely of me.

Validation of a Good Man

୧୧୧

He gently wipes away all her painful tears,

His heart attentively listens to occupied fears,

Comforting words through lips with a soothing deep voice,

Freeing her from shadow's imprisonment of one's choice,

Gazing through her eyes, refraining from taking
this moment in vain,

Disclosing past men's selection, vowing non-production
from prolonging pain;

Open arms offering entrance is within
his safe haste ground,

Affectionate validation of a good man
has finally been found,

She now walks in confidence, clasping each experience
with vigorous manner,

Rejecting hesitation his government last name
became her imprinted banner,

Acknowledging what truly found this woman was of
honesty sealed love,

Heart's companion issuance came from
the Heavenly Father up above.

The Comprehension

ଅଅଅ

Considering examination in the direction of your eyes,

Quality possessed by existence towards
today/tomorrow/and my future lies,

Restituting pleasure as an attribution of a woman's heart,

Limiting negation her conveying means
conditioned lengths to depart;

She withholds compliance of granted position
as his second choice,

Walls form while intentions disregard exhausted cries
from her trembling voice;

He lacks qualifications in the main body of
communicating matter,

Disposition enclosing wealth's understanding within
compulsion prosperity to shatter,

Reject one's feeling of great displeasure for love
deteriorated in me;

His responsibility descended defeat from heart
enabling naked eye to see,

Delaying my true value by solely ignoring
the human mental state of mind,

Absent presence embraces changing lanes towards an
appreciative kind,

Standing in darkness as shadows of imprinted
comprehension leaves him with regret,

He now realizes the traces of her sweet aroma
lingering in space stigmatized to never forget.

The Exquisite Key

෧෧෧

She obstructed the view of sentiments hidden
by her captivating smile,

Transitory nation couldn't comprehend one's crosses
at any given mile,

Her muscle strength appeared just a simple mirage
through clear window panes;

Thoughts held the mind prisoner behind repetitive flashes
of unforgotten lanes,

Turning off emotions, shielding her heart
from enemies in fight,

Wisdom partakes towards understanding acquired through
a stroking flare of light;

Enduring love by yourself is a costly place to even reside,

As she burn at moderate intensity liberating tenderness
inward slide,

Freedom from exertion her arm coincide partly
with darkened weary eyes,

Inhaling natural currents of air
as the time vigorously flies,

Acknowledging diamonds' honest value
towards her true desire,

Acceptance for character possessed is the exquisite key
all sincerely admire,

Exhaling all stimulated tension restrained from loving
anyone from afar,

Contemplating with faith as the ball of light
reflected upon the star,

Being in an upright supported position with
excessive self-assurance ardent,

Without delay she's prevalent to cognizant
as distinguished high ranking sergeant.

Distinctive Desires

ଵଵଵ

Tongues of light emitted from wax as we stood
countenance to face,

His embracement affected emotions in arousal
towards a sweet, enamored place:

Gently reclining, descending control tender lips
he passionately kissed,

Heavy hands glide down physical structure
no curve was perceptively missed,

Eliminating entrance light she slowly inhales
captive moment's time;

Depth of his moan rings through her ears
like the single awakening chime,

Particular mind eluded in third gear as one's atmosphere
deviates from afar,

He angled from upright position conferring her strong
inclination upon a star,

Consummate me with benevolence absorbed
throughout your heart's loyalty,

I will reciprocate your devotional stand as mere
high valued price of royalty,

Exhaling to alleviate mental bondage held
from deep inside her walls,

Now the trumpet of roar possessed by character
is what he solely calls,

One's body opposed to solid surface erasing all bonded
lustful distinctive desire,

All consumed without reservation in her soul
set suitable conscious on fire,

With exhaustion their frames to pillow fall
imprinted indentions of time,

Appreciating what appeared in light will form
higher price than a dime.

A Man's Regretful Heart

ରୁରୁ

Meditating distinction by losing comprehensibility
of her desiring thirst,

Omitting in subdivision obligation to interpose
his woman first,

She intolerantly positioned anticipating your arrival
with admiration by minute of hand,

Presence was occupied deceitfully enclosed
by fruit on a forbidden land,

Isn't that some love to feel betrayal walk through
unadorned hollowed door?

She boldly rises upon her feet issuing a sweet kiss
and stressing softly "no more."

For in one's heart there weren't any comparative towards
collard greens/cornbread/and sweet potato pie,

Submission towards brothel's lure appeared intently
valuable enough to place a temporary high,

Drowning in his sea of anguish presently acknowledging
she won't ever overcome,

He is just a man left with regretful distressing heart
pondering, where will love reappear from?

Seeing her face is like two ships passing
in the midnight hour towards now,

Just to lay his emotions in her hands there is no way
or entrance of questioning how.

Hands of Time

ඉඉඉ

Internal needs toward lowering head
as she voluntarily closes her eyes,

Thoughts of disreputable days danced in darkness
while path from history flies,

Issuance intensified attention if one could create life
at origin or alter anything,

Expression of desire questioned scars from misuse outlined
character's reproach to sing,

Strength sustained for directions love or hate me
concerning departure remained in your heart,

I am ever so grateful towards given trials of branded
torment that kept us apart,

Educated experiences evolving reprimand transforming
ownership was sincerely positioned,

Acknowledging her true worth's value with one's heart
deserving to be conditioned,

You were my purpose and tunnels traveling tribulation
of bolted flashing lights,

The joy in rising sun that lifted my stand towards
all battling striven fights,

Objective of individuality resides in me peacefully
captivating another chime,

She now sits represented graciously refusing one
to change the hands of time.

Cherished in Eternity

୧୧୧

Drifting eyes in pillowing spaces pounding time
to make a change,

Patiently I await my reward as one sits from afar in range,

Deserving inward deep reception of something
well-spoken and committed,

My heart you stand firm while one entirely sits submitted,

Aches and pains warned out in despair as her heart
became eventually broken,

Not acknowledging one's value is more costly than some
solid mattered token,

Woman's worth consists within limits of love
she has to even give,

Longing to be cherished in eternity as truly respected
and freely live,

Contemplating deep within thoughts striking bolts
come straight to head,

We all are assumingly human deserving towards having
heart and soul constantly fed.

The Profundity

ｅｅｅ

Standing motionless before image in reflective glass and
what do I see?

Weighing mind towards representation forming
her strength or is it just me?

Drawing inferences of long causes in journeyed roads
and all my tears,

Comprehension able me to smile validating footprints
stamped faithfully through the years,

Sole purpose of adoration towards providing exigency
with respect to be compromised,

Once sincerity closed doors the love in heart freed
obstruction was clearly visualized,

Presently indicative love in distance being one's lingering
dream with his heart is exceedingly real,

Consistency of piercing through my structured frame
outlines the profundity I assumingly feel.

Opportunity Missed

☙☙☙

She went lurking for true love in all the wrong places,

Proceeding directional steps towards invisible
contoured traces,

Impatiently awaiting a visual message
appearing from deep within me,

One's unveiling of his heart ambled her
to finally feel and clearly see,

Sincerity approached in assortment with various kinds
with consistent disguises—

The single far most bold heading that she
momentarily realizes,

Precise opportunity has been missed to even experience
one's heartfelt love,

Installments of gifts were voluntarily
refunded/walking/and throwing surrendered hands above.

Taking Control

೨೨೨

*C*autiously awaiting the arrival of altercating matter
in time's origin that may come,

Questioning neglect towards whence destination
had even departed from,

Requirements of deleting family and friends surrounding
life's formed in rearrange,

Demanding illness mode for directional peaceful habitat
with existence creative change,

Assumingly there is any who seek out to decisively
keep her at any united force,

Visible presence effortlessly appeared obsolete
in her time of deficiency source,

To permit them emotional control over mental state
of mind from what she truly deserve,

Granting one within limits near vaulted happiness
towards positioning joy on reserve,

The indefinite extent during existence release
joined control setting forth her smile,

Remoting regions from one who lacks judgment,
she disjointed by a calculated mile.

Significance of Perception

𝕖𝕖𝕖

Unerring integrity for appropriate attainment towards
possession of love sustains in me,

Refrain from representing masking of hardness
as if the naked eye can't even see,

Evil's rooted value is one's false conception to ever
conquer her heart,

The impersonation reflected counterfeit strength
resulting into rending two apart,

Contemplation towards heartache questioned mind
if he only had one single clue,

Committed love permitted any man of lustful bargaining
entrance to astray from you,

Understanding change within me formed dominating
utterance in directional trials and crosses,

Grasp the significance of perception from existence
or one will process numerous losses.

Prevailing Elevation

ଏଏଏ

Calculation of time is near and the exact change
has finally come,

Maturity lines with prosperity given is exactly
where it appeared from,

Observation of who have befitted in one's mind
remained a one-sided mystery;

Please draw a little closer toward my heart
recognize repeated time to history,

The Source of mother in direction of daughter's reflection
she can precisely see—

Validation possessed by beauty enclosed her life's
captivation directly into me,

Within her upward path's walk all structure transformed
upright and strong,

Escorting steps mildly across the obstacles,
hurdling miles viewed utterly long,

Head securely held in elevation above weapons formed
from one's inner core,

Controlling darkness hands of defeat
she won't have to even withstand anymore.

Defining Love

ଏଏଏ

Love is not an infectious virus that penicillin can
treat or even cure,

Its artillery's present indicative choice enclosed by
inherent heart constructed feeling sure,

Emotion is extraordinary exception in ability forming an
indivisible linguistic unit expressed,

Without precise timing conveying whatever quality or
characteristics momentarily stress,

Enticing hastily temptation's enamored taste of silky
smoothness of flowing wine,

The support in affliction moderately embracing scars
altering everything to be fine,

If profound affection allows free passages consisting spaces
to continuously question why,

Then give intense attention towards how deep
devotion intentionally hover you by.

Mother's Non-Refundable Love

ৡৡৡ

$\mathcal{A}$ mother's deep emotion cannot be
refunded or traded in,

Trapping of nerves result to breathing deep
then counting to ten;

No matter the aggravation in picture
she truly means you well,

Her love is one visualized intensively
for one can honestly tell,

If knowledge ever lacked towards what appeared
in direction of being the best,

Mother's inner strength would be put forth
to acquired equivalency test,

Considering validation toward life's escalating expectation
exalting far above,

Acknowledging through exhausted cry is the official
summoned translation of love.

The Forbidden Rose

ଶଶଶ

She walks in alluring darkness pleasing to the
widening of his eyes,

Seductively hips sway back and forth as hypnotizing
aroma in cursory motion flies,

Lusting for her juices of nectar from the shadowing
widow's authorized deceit,

Disregarding purity acres on fruitful surface whom
possesses his legal certified receipt,

Weakening submission towards betrayal slowly lowers
numbing frame into woven weave of death,

Heart submerges emotional artifice in directional amnesia
obtaining white rose's initial taken breath,

Requirements effortlessly demand catering to two roses
leaving unbalanced habituation scars,

Finally recognizing symbolic extraneous contamination
she hung your footprints to represent stars,

He strongly contemplates on the forbidden rose and its
costly exertion state of venue,

Acknowledging being in love with two flowers wasn't worth
engorging guile on any sort of menu.

Emotional Rollercoaster

ଐଐଐ

You are the blood that pumps my heart to beat,
The vocal call towards responsive rise upon my feet,

Breath's traveling cause resulting exhalation
breathing so deep,

The words of consummation motioning me
to peacefully sleep,

You are my consolation that gently wipes away the tears,

Security embracement that armored me from
cradling fears,

You are the nutrition to my soul that fills me up,

The sweet taste of wine overflowing my
emotional rimmed cup,

You are the gentle touch that calms
my raging storm's nerve,

That sets inward well-spoken expression
in me on preserve,

There's no need towards response or focus on one's
sincere words as a second look,

This is not poetry to be quietly edited inside of my
Unspoken Heart book—

It's also a mere melody that flowed
at the awakening of my day,

In order to share what you do for me
in every sense of one's way.

Documented Memory

୧୧୧

*H*astily she outlined the progress of his vigorous
seductive manner in walk,

Beholding muscular abdomen captivated vision
enabling her to even talk,

Issuing heed towards drawled concentration from
deepening roar of one's vocal tone,

Climate in atmosphere altered appearing as if occupancy
consumed they were all alone,

Leisurely mannered approach positioned their
mesmerizing rituality of motion locking hands,

Focusing on inward depths from his alluring eyes had her
hydroplaning on silky sands,

He outlined the contour for her shapely frame without
any pauses toward one's unspoken spaces,

Mental images followed his steps within direction assuring
non-mistakable radiant lines of traces,

She gently elevates his head bringing forth attention
to meet her rounded face,

While one's voice whispered winds of sentiment
through tender hearted lips towards embrace,

Seizing each timely moment as a valuable auctioned piece
priced on a plat-form stage,

Has thoughts noted in documented memory of turning
each journey to their own edited page.

The Cold Room

ରରର

Placing one foot in front of the other,

Questioning, "Is it more to life than being a mother?"

Entering my room I sadly look around:

All in me suddenly hit solid ground,

Feeling of emptiness filled my space,

No one here to give a comforting embrace,

Just to have someone here greeting with a smile,

Making coming home each night worth my mile,

To draw me in with a passionate kiss,

Assuring with touch my presence he miss,

Saying I love you as music to my ear,

Making me feel inside his heart is always near

Arms wrapping weary body not letting go,

Do I say enough? Please, I don't think so!

He massages my muscles, applying silky cream,

Eyes relaxed closed for a fallen dream,

As I turn over and take this moment in,

Vision open wide then whisper up to ten,

In sight nothing has truly begin to bloom,

All dwelling here is just a dreary cold room.

The Open Door

೮೮೮

*L*owering body with arms positioned behind me,

Wind swiftly whispering taking in what the eye can see,

Mind shift to first gear, filling with thoughts of you,

Falling in love again has heart consumed with fear too,

Never imagined the sun would ever shine my way,

Thunderstorms and pains branded each passing day,

Unstoppable dreams I gave up on long ago,

Every man that entered drifted in winds to blow,

You came knocking passionately on my front door,

Walls could not withstand loneliness no more,

As you opened my heart sparing your last dime,

I stood cautiously to grab love one more time.

Daddy's Little Girl

ଽଽଽ

Taking in arm the gift he embraces,

All envisioned is of innocence trace,

Emotional connection brings smiling joy

It's his little girl and not a toy,

Becoming her father appears in a dream.

Does he maintain or start to scream?

Leaning down he softly places a kiss,

Each tender moment he don't attempt to miss,

In time without intention he applies the scar,

Her bond with him will come from afar,

Every failed relationship result from wounds in life,

Naïve for love instills stabbing infliction of a knife,

Becoming a woman and to stand her ground,

Has heart's past loneliness lurking all around,

Will a man ever dance with his daughter
in happiness twirl?

For the feeling has expired to become daddy's little girl.

My Desire

㉔㉔㉔

Opening her eyes to the morning light,

No apparent muscle throughout her is tight,

Breathing deeply inward freed of one's stressed,

Not wanting movement or attempt to get dressed,

Reminiscing on a long night's romancing story,

Passionate bond released in mind her worry,

His affection destroyed all solid walls,

Echoes in the room is his name of vocal calls,

Heaviness of his hands is a message he send,

This moment of luxury she never wants to end,

Arms pulling her close not letting go,

In heart she wants to love him so,

Turning head over to now an empty space,

All imprinted sheets lined in his body trace,

Looking over a text from the long mile,

Words expressed raise her teenage glowing smile,

For all that he has to offer is an admire,

Standing to acknowledge that he is what her heart desires.

Missed Out

ରରର

He stood tall with piercing hazel eyes,

Locked at sight she felt connection, but why?

No one could halt attention or break her down,

His walk of confidence had fear with a frown,

Drawing her in towards all he possess:

Originality and personality one had to confess,

Friendship was not enough in satisfying her emotion,

Hardness weakened for his heart's devotion,

Eyes hungered filled with tears longing pain,

Struggling fear of loving him drove her insane,

At moments end she forced to open up,

Stepping forward like one scared little pup,

Feeling his response with her begin to fold,

Temperatures no longer sensing hot but cold,

Expressing all within her of regretful reject,

His death ears turned from past neglect,

The man meant for her is gone due to denial,

Digits of his number she can't even redial.

He Loves Me Not

ଅଅଅ

Waking up beside him makes best part of day,

Smile enlarges parted lips from tender words he say,

Heaviness of his hands glide gently up and down one side,

The depth of her breath exhale to expansions wide,

Motioning her flat placing fingers on the hips,

Leaning downward he begins making love to her lips,

This morning, time is only hanging by a thin thread,

As her long, silky legs begin to slowly spread,

Expressions from mouth stressed words of love,

Surroundings of empty responses to her lying above,

Eyes wide shut, deep down, her heart knew
he was the one,

Or was she fresh meat for him to just have fun?

Pushing him off all emotions inside went numb,

Last thing he remembered up in air her finger
and not a thumb.

One with You

ଽଽଽ

The night slept away as we silently lay,

Never imagine moments like this to come my way,

Fate won't turn back the hands of time,

Sweet music through ears slowly chimes,

We've stolen each morning forgetting about tomorrow,

Belonging to me sweet nights your heart I borrow;

We should had counted up all of our priceless cost,

Instead, in midst of the hours our minds were lost,

My heart refuses for you to even see—

How loving him is gradually killing me,

Not wanting more than to be part of your life,

Carrying his last name by making me the wife,

One look in your eyes and I can clearly see,

How much this man truly means to me;

His love is all happiness should be consisted of,

No denying what I feel not even to the man above,

He got me doing things never in thought I would ever do,

Just wanting to be one with him instead of
feeling like number two.

Black-Out

ରରର

Stretched with dry waterfalls lined down her pale face,

Silver metal content laid upon as a temporary place,

Attempting to retract how one landed a cold room:

Visions in head are blurry with outlines of gloom,

Surrounding echo voices speaking from
medical terms of technology;

She did not go to college, but one appeared
degree of biology,

White covering shield blocking optical sight,

All is not dark for there's a faded gleaming light,

Footsteps are to pavement as temperature
never begin to change;

She can't feel a heartbeat for no emotion is in range,

A hand lowers to head removing cloth of protection,

In glass above mounted flat one mirrored reflection,

Eyes positioned towards the ceiling
without a minute's blink,

Now being motionless, she won't have to even think,

The face is unrecognizable for any human being to see,

I'm lying lifeless because he took all his anger out on me.

Irreversible Love

ତ୍ତ୍ତ୍

*H*ead to window eyes pierced gazing up in air,

Mind contemplating time without a moment in despair,

Never knowing my heart would ever sing
a brand new song,

Through the falling waters fate brought you along,

He revealed another piece of me that I would never
break his heart,

Vowing my love is solid and irreversibly do us part,

Entering my life you molded all in me anew,

Proven your ground as man desires becoming
one with you,

Through your storms I'll take your hand
and together we'll fight,

Trust troubles don't last always, we will endure only
for a night,

Babe, you are my guiding heart and I your shining star,

No matter how overwhelming time emerges
my love is never far.

Lonely Heart

ᘒᘒᘒ

Standing still in mirrored reflection at longing glance,

Mesmerizing heart's reason of loneliness
with given chance,

Exhausted of games that lead to all traveling dead ends,

She's done all from past in words to make a total mends,

Realizing everyone surrounding her has each other's heart,

I'm visualized a mere mirage in darkness
that tears me apart,

Values built inside at offerings costly stake,

Shielded walls caused response motioning huge mistake,

Finally in love led me to opening the front door,

Honestly speaking I just can't handle being alone no more,

What does it take getting the message to him
clearly through?

My heart aching from needing/missing/and
being in love with you.

Shadow Disguising

ଚ୍ଚ୍ଚ

Walking straight in form standing six feet tall,

On guard with armor to everyone's pleading call,

He's a mere man in the silent shadows of disguise,

Don't let anyone fool you this one is very wise,

Approaching devil's advocates without a bit of fear,

When in pursuit still waters divide systematically clear,

Vicious with his calm toned words cutting hands of time,

Causing herd to spread at the drop of a dime,

Some misconstrue his shiftiness sharpening of the eye,

As strength in wind confidentially flew us by,

Be aware of passing on wrongful crossing roads,

Whether justice or injustice his heart sustain
balancing all loads,

The men honored motto defend and protect
requires no tool,

He stands boldly armored as the sitting "PITBULL".

Acceptance

৭৭৭

$\mathcal{L}$ooking into his eyes, thinking developmental trust,

Meeting each other half way has to be a must,

Contemplating at times she don't appreciate all that he do,

Not knowing what it takes getting through to you,

Acknowledging her heart by neglecting one's pride,

He's giving you his all to stand by your side,

Realizing she may be asking of you too much,

All needed is your tender loving touch,

Remember we were friends before becoming lovers,

No need to concentrate on actions intercepting of others,

She can't hold back her feelings of wanting
to be your woman now,

Everything in you she hungers for so take a bow,

Don't turn away from what you made in her stronger,

The solid walls that was built stands visible no longer,

Do not worry about her ever wanting you to leave,

Lay down your head and my heart
with open arms receives.

Fading Away

ଶ ଶ ଶ

She halts in front of windows light,

Exhausting towards outer viewing sight,

Mind compacted with situations that are subterfuge,

Boy, you got her soul bounded and so confused,

Heart's truth's standing hardened to believe,

Guarded walls broken open arms in trials receive,

Realizing without you she's hopelessly lost,

Vowing her will to reign no matter what the cost,

Not wanting to be without his presence
from blinding years,

Thinking of him constantly fills eyes towards
pouring tears,

Being in love has one desiring more,

She's offering her all; please don't walk out that door,

Not having much of anything if there's no existence of you,

Past mistakes was made for her heart had not a clue,

She's fighting with what's left in her on fallen knee,

Acknowledging all you are to her she can finally see,

Visualizing him fading in thin, cold air,

What was once seen from you is no longer there.

Fist Full of Tears

෧෧෧

The mind is racing compacted with trials of life,

Heartaches sending blows pulsating levels
from one's strife,

Her soul is darkened from shadows lurking all round,

Lips frozen stiff, restricting developmental form of sound,

Questioning paths bad seed from whence one sow,

Wounds and scars which is of deserving,
she just don't know,

Exhausted: body falls numb on blanketed sand,

Focusing towards dancing ocean waves
as an orchestrated band,

Winds softly massaging her face while it flows swiftly by,

Temporarily comforting her inward spirits
as briskly time fly,

Remembering shared time together and
joy he bought to her heart,

Misconception of her words resulted in tearing them apart,

Emptiness fills her life at the silence of his voice,

Being treated as an auctioned valued item
withheld from her choice,

Yearning for his love he kept her placement confused,

Past image of offerings is what drawled her
completely amused,

His hand slowly faded as towards love grew even stronger,

The man who hungered her in desire existed no longer,

Spaded cards flipped as the guarded gate opened wide,

Assuming through everything he would
remain by one side,

All appears a nightmare for he always
imprinted her smile,

In need of his embrace from misconception
in distancing mile,

Gradually she gently opens the eyes as
inward beginning fears,

Looking down in her hands embraced was a
fist full of tears.

Killing Me Softly

ඒඒඒ

Lying with back on top of one's empty bed,

Thoughts bounded losing him heavily dance in her head,

Consuming muscles inward is blood flowing fear,

Pillow soaking holding every heartfelt tear,

Woman dwelled inside still branded in me,

As I place arms across my face, so reality won't see,

Consumed inside that you don't even love me the same,

My broken expectations is unaware towards
who's to blame,

So I will just lay here, drowning in emptiness
of my sorrow,

Reluctant to visions one have facing for tomorrow,

Minutes passing slowly, killing her softly
not hearing his voice,

Visual words would at least give heart reason
to rise and rejoice,

Deep down, Self did not want to believe directional clue,

All imprisoned in me with the way "I truly love you."

.

Thinking of your absent presence is a high price to pay,

One will do what it takes inside to remain all the way.

The form you entered is needed and she sincerely miss,

Desire is to run in your arms and to your lips
to place a gentle kiss,

Slowly opening her eyes, turning where he once abide,

Wishing you was here, pulling me closely to your side.

Numbing Pain

ଯ ଯ ଯ

Slowly lowering weary body across her bed,

Tilting head on hands tears begin to downward shed,

No knowledge could explain inside how she truly feel,

Reminiscing words piercing from his tongue
like a legal seal,

Her mind two steps toward days only one can fantasize,

Visions of absence and silence she motion to realize,

Him, after timely years, not feeling her by now,

This man will never love her no way or how,

She turns over as eyes blink towards moments spark,

Astonished in wonder the months placed
he had one in dark,

Softly whispering this is not how I'm known to be,

All the loves she have for him has
consummation of jealousy,

He should had left her in landing comfort
where she belong,

Deception of misleading to his emotional belief was wrong,

She possessed all control for her path without
taking all in vain,

Now one has to struggle each day,
coping another numbing pain.

A Shadow's Missing Link

୧୧୧

Sternly walking she halts facing wooded support to rest,

Young mind pressure lacks all understanding
to his unanswered test,

Innocence for world's entrance was uncontrolled
by no choice,

Impact of daddy's emotional lashes left her
numbing corded voice,

Remembering trafficking tears falling at star
glaring night,

Needing daddy's love towards standing ground
to defend and fight,

Conscientious steps aside boldly placing hand on hip,

Speaking firmly, "Strength come landing on
your tongues tip."

Realize whose foundation Heavenly Father
truly consisted of,

His unconditioned love never abandons,
not even from above,

So go wash the waters stains from material pillow form,

Place your daddy name in Word for it's his dwelling storm,

Focus solely on growth passage, but don't act
before you timely think,

Reframe all actions of past for he is child's
shadow's missing link.

The Bonding Reflection

୧୧୧

The head on hand while she lay is gently placed,

Tears filled her eyes blocking visions as if one
had been maced,

Heart beat slowly weakened at missing time lost,

Having her uncle near appraised value of no pricey cost,

Explanation is not required for gaps bonding spaces,

Your niece's engraved love towards you is like
woven shoe laces,

Her mirrored reflection colored eyes was
inherited from you,

So when standing in glass to shave, you will see me too,

Just lean a little closer and focus towards clarifying face,

My smile shows the joy within direction's trace,

Now I lower my lids fading out all brightening light,

Dreaming running in your arms and my uncle
holding me real tight,

So when you lay in darkness contemplating on how
I have grown,

Don't forget all memories we had stored
never to be thrown,

The little girl that you last look upon with me
one captivating smile,

Is a grown woman whose love is closer than
any distant mile?

She's keeping in visual every card you sent,

If you thought it was trash, you got me bent,

Cherishing every word within each single one
personally to cater,

So with me there's no goodbye; it's always I see you later.

Hidden Heart's Depression

୧୧୧

In her bed with cover over the face,

Body laying numb while heartbeats slow in pace,

Head tilted to the side on silky pillow coldness touch,

Mind overwhelmed with questions why she cared so much,

He came as a dream that shielded from all her pain,

Disguised in visual luxury given herself to him
was all in vain,

Now she lays drowning all torn down from
his defamation ways,

All wasted time cherished demolished in calculated days,

Reoccurrence is what she kept hidden
from childhood fears,

The scars reopened after falsifying documents
erased trusted years,

Her emotions are confused withdrawn to state of mind,

Unaware he possessed character of the
unconscientiously kind,

Despite his actions not considering her true emotions,

Blinded to her love for him and hearted devotions,

She will never forget the moment of his first tender kiss,

For in him what was valuable memory she truly miss,

Mind just visualizes how it all in wind just flies,

Deepening of her pain refuses the heart to say goodbye,

He walked away as if nothing ever really mattered,

Just turned his morals leaving her life totally shattered,

So she closes out all surroundings just wanting
to be left alone,

No sound is welcomed not even the ringing of her phone,

Now closing saddened eyes to block out all captured light,

She places hand on chest for her heart can't
endure this fight,

All spoken words of what this woman truly deserved,

The imprint is only of an expired label preserved.

Struggling Devoid of Light

⊝⊝⊝

Look in her shallow eyes, the message runs skin deep,

Tender lips pressed is like a child who quietly weeps,

In need of having enormous bond absented within vitality,

Expressing possibility of desire from direction
confining reality,

Her soul loudly calls out intensely producing
a shadow of bond,

Heart falls beneath still waters as solid rock propelled
through pond,

Her compacted conscious matured weary within
misleading blinded sight,

Acknowledging developed strength from one's
struggling devoid of light,

Bombarding any man out of entering heart
with folded arms to defeat,

She realizes underserving scars endured her value
he did so cheat,

Head stiffly turned right and leaned toward imprinted
degree of no fear,

She stands boldly in defense while keeping her
Heavenly Father near.

The Reconstruction

ରରର

Calmly sitting gazing towards brightness in the sky,

Contemplating how digital numerals just clocked us by,

Unaware of future moldings characterized
possessing deep inside,

Capturing keepsake moments of growth taken for a ride,

Fork in roads intercepted dreams with
reverence order issue,

Leaving one alone swallowing in regret tightly
clenching pillowed tissue,

Acknowledging wisdoms growth by forgiveness
of human painful tears,

All had taken enduring rollercoaster turns up and down
throughout timely years,

Slowly bowing his head the hands firmly
embracing a single hold,

For it is now he realizes his life in desperate
reconstruction of a mold,

The love built within his heart has graphically represented
gestational change,

Comprehending methodically endearment of others
non-restrictive range,

When period of light between rising and setting
of the sun appear,

Keep in repository of cognition of one's ardor is
in-variably near.

Land of Deliverance

୧୧୧

*H*e sits stiffly without shiftiness of an eye,

Observing each human as they quickly moved by,

Impacting in hearts is power of his light,

Refusing rest until over life's cultivating fight,

Tightly folding arms without one bit of fear,

Visible sound for tearful cries echoing extremely near,

Walking with confidence he halts to her pain,

Gently lifting her face assuring all won't be in vain,

All she has to do is have faith and accept his hand,

He promises sweet melody with deliverance of land,

She is clueless the message this one has to send,

In him all apparent is heart's threaded needle mend,

Through green fields they stroll without any worries;

Now her soul is fully preserved of untold stories,

Taking charitable moments she sealed to her heart,

Stamped with love that no man can ever tear apart.

To Always Abide

ହ ହ ହ

Gentle words from his tender lips comforted me
through the times of troubling despair,

One's visible presence slowly eased my fears like
softening touching breeze within midnight air,

Sharpened piercing eyes strongly signaled one's soul
that his hear would never go astray,

From each answered call that was made completed
a prone fact he wasn't too far away,

The touch of his heavy hands that glided against mine
guaranteeing I was kept safe at home,

True assurance of each waking time with one trip
or stumble notarized she wasn't left alone,

He soothingly embraced my every depressing trials
and firmly catches me when I fall,

Firmly issuing his hones consolation while unselfishly
supplying from within his all,

As he gently wiped all my painful tears away promising
to remain always by one's side,

Validating seal verified that he's sincerely here dwelling
with me in revolving times to always abide.

Beauty of Existence

ଚ୍ଚି

Smoothness of complexion exposes one's vision
in reflection constituting chalky coal,

Her imposing character is directed towards emotion that
comforts the engrossed soul,

Aiding thoroughly morbid living body contributing
consolation as insisted blanketed shape,

Patience adhered to every tearful waking call issuing
calming calculations with associating escape,

Softly spoken words sweetened as if gradually melting
each one's tender heart,

Negative lashes of weapons she prohibited admittance
towards tearing integrity apart,

Walking across green pasture's acre gliding inward
sexuality as abiding attributing grace,

No attention of man's revolving head while the minute
hand outlined time's shadowing trace,

Decorated hard back cover disguised literature's
significance stabilizing morality in park,

Actual solutions to artistic visual qualities are held within
beautiful pictures developed amongst the dark.

Black Widow

ଉ ଉ ଉ

Woman of Perfection carefully examining prey with
macabre behavior towards quenching thirst,

Surveying blue printed surroundings infatuation
is becoming as far as her character first,

Transformation hates loathing darkness deceitfulness
of one's dark beautified kind,

Singularly possesses heartless violent ritual while
predatory towards men she subsequently find,

Carefully sketching out motion purposed in organized
itinerary for her magnetizing lure,

Obsessively articulating every inch within symmetry
mansion's potion desiring to be sure,

Blindfolding in trance from her mental block towards
successful fertilization,

Puncturing his heart with digestive enzymes liquidized
one into past due realization,

Silky legs unwrapped his body freeing out of placement
presence never again to reside,

Leaving behind questionable shadowing spaces lusted in
tears craving essence losing all his pride,

Teenage past tense innocence of valuable virgin jewel
selfishly the father did so take,

Now revenging beautiful black widow presents laughter of
kneading her men into one well rounded flat crab cake.

Sensual Potion

ଉଉଉ

$\mathcal{S}$teaming water pours aimlessly toward solid white
structure as rose petals move swiftly in moderate motions,

Guiding into position, gently he massages feet exposing
true deep relaxing introduction of his inward devotion,

Eyes are filled with silent unspoken sense as one leans
inward placing upon lips a sweet tender kiss,

Alluring vision glares directly in hers expressing
nonresident duration towards calculation he truly miss

Gently hand glides against innocent face while inhalation
becomes soothing therapy's aroma candle scent,

Acknowledging the want of easing all one's pain by
outward extension from his forelimbs he so invitingly lent,

Frigidly lifting, handling with care as elevation enclosed
one by openly contributing being her breakfast in bed,

Cogitating a good man right before her presence after
experiencing pain is an outward speech well said,

Visual smile placed on her face develops into yearning for
one's sincere loving touch of soul mates embrace,

Captivating scent from his sensual potion has sweet
lingering morning winds blowing an unforgettable trace.

Behind the Masking Smile

෧෧෧

Unaccompanied in secluded space consciousness escaped
ones of unobtrusive sorted kind,

In visions smile she conveyed gratification to surround
souls inspiring unenclosed within mind,

Altering shadows endured on the farther side of her eyes
towards abundant unveiling stories,

Recognized for one's upright position as single mother
clearly portrayed pictures engrossing no worries,

Visions naked frontage was supplied by her enlightening
issuance during moments of misery time,

Vocal tones translated form, becoming transparent echoes
from her vibrating laughter as resonate existing chime,

Deep bondage possessed by lamenting adolescence
intensifying desire to assassinate entirety fears,

The earnest of one's sincerity towards representation
devoting his emotional warmth annihilating tears,

Extensions route to love self-formed strength as a
solid shield, rejecting all within she longed for,

Painful scars from deceitful hands of manipulation
hindered comfort zone in security lands
and valuing towards more,

Voluntarily she auctions oneself to be deprived from
rightful royalties through a centered traveling mile.

A Mother's Devotional Love

୧୧୧

Looking down at your face questioning
what could one even do?

Wishing if I could just take all pain and suffering
completely out of you,

Vowing as your mother, one's side never to
medically neglect or even leave,

For the flashbacks of your sweet angeled brother
still so numbingly do I grieve,

Bowing my head, praying each day God's hand
solidly remains bonded onto you,

Assuring one thing is known of our Father's love
it remains completely true,

Battling fight we are in together no matter what
to our visual way may come,

No one can separate my devotion and strength
or question where it's from,

All that I have sacrificed is due to one's love and
commitment to all my kids,

Feria/Duetch Marks/or De Nero it doesn't matter what
for I take no bids,

My stats a devoted mother is instilled through life
and until trials end,

Even there do I never stop for far above the eldest one
my love I do so send,

Now your mother is here to do all one can accomplish
with entirety within me,

To all of no understanding of heart in my place towards
them I do now see,

Here one stand for her children she carried that are legally
notarized as mine,

Beware of inward crossings for karma in return don't taste
sweet as soothing wine.

The Game

ଵଵଵ

Stepping out showering mist the toning muscles
rejuvenate towards moistening watered massage,

Clearing reflective glass from steaming fog admiring
his mere simplified conceited mirage,

Cockiness kept silk of coolness against one's back while he
deposited ends into Armani's pocket,

Alluring appearance booked women's asset towards
electrifying insertion to his magnetizing socket,

Childhood scars molded from mothering neglect indulged
sweet self-unconscious revenging drive,

Approaching like the bull to matador his passionate brown
sugar hypnotized women's high thrusting thrive,

Contractual thinning between happiness and anger
numbingly stamped his singular numbered code,

Vowing to never speak words of emotion barricading
heart's feelings by setting costly but valuable mode,

Fulfilling each woman's night with his shadows
from deception branding their lifetime towards pain,

The game clarified powerful form of lions' demeanor in
strut as heartless blood flowing vein.

The Mere Illusion

ହହହ

She graciously stood before one's presence heightened
in patenting black leather stiletto heels,

His motioning command formed eyes lustful pleasures
while the drawled attention she inward reels,

He became her decimal loving touch of sensation that is
greater in velocity than one had ever truly known;

No superior situation was preferred losing evolving control
but through aura on leisure's own

Gentle kiss rested upon the forehead clearly signifying
sweet endearment and all he was of,

Deep strengthening warmth towards affection remained as
uninterrupted lavational breaths exceeding above,

His sensual aromatherapy placed her soul into overdrive,
igniting one's raging pulsation on fire,

Leaving indicative disagreement's space for conferring
ground rules within entirety desire,

Arms stretching outward with an inclinational arch
in back while eyes opened up to her brightened
morning light,

Revolving head towards vacant sack filled cushion she
realizes he was the mere illusion of imagination for
captivity's night.

Mi Hermana Hermosa

ଵଵଵ

Laying exhausted frame on top of solid resting ground
her wounded soul painfully weeps,

Head heavily buried into one's folded arms as waterfalls
pour until thought silently sleeps,

Awakening to the morning rise standing upright
taking each motioning steps in prayerful stride,

Appearance towards mirrored glass reflection revealed
a woman's retrieval strength of molded pride,

Validating direction by refusing allowanced rights
her emotion take full control valuing justified life,

Demanding reprimand of good offerings from mortal man
she cut deception with a jagged edged knife,

One's heart consumed the monetary merit that flowed
inward compliment's radiant creditability's smile;

Descriptive wording can't define her joyful issuance
in displayed dimples through passing mile,

Wanting the luxury for my sister's life as a superstar
she would be supplied the want and need,

Never neglecting one minute of hand by assuring her of
being beautiful came as her imprinted seed.

Questionable Intentions

ଉଉଉ

$\mathcal{B}$oldly presenting himself solid form towards her
knight's protective shining armor of venue,

Smooth vinyl words flowed through his lips, portraying
succulent steak on any expensive menu,

Tormented beyond poisoned scars deceitful hands
hardened her heart into a strict barrier wall,

The fear within embraced living in taunting of shadows
of refusing love's singular intensified call,

Importance of feelings is to revolve one's world solely
towards revealing our deepening soul's impression,

Don't create assumptions merely based upon questionable
intentions for betrayal's seeking depression,

She don't need her universe evolving in circular motion
surrounding his planet's residing towards space,

Man of destination offerings in search of his queen
vanished upon her arms' surrounding pace,

Yielding heart issued to man representing all deity
dispersed without a conscious simplifying outlined trace,

She interrogated handing the direction for emotion's state
of imprisonment regarding her heart,

Vividly delivering routed awareness order towards wasted
recurring time deemed necessary to depart.

The Chase

ଥାଏ

Resting head in one's arm as she silently listens to heart
beating sounds while they exhaustingly rest,

Focusing towards painted walls lips part fearlessly as she
whispers "I love you" setting emotional test,

Slowly turning his face with shifting eyes leaving echoes
speechless from hollowed shadowing space,

Rays of light awakens her lusting blindness for comfort
with his presence vacated envisioned place,

Realizing in documented memories that she had
transformed into his convenient beck and call,

Merely clarified sight of one's self-righteous clothing made
her rapid running water downward fall,

Consumed configuration would be moments directed
towards no matter of emotional legalized care,

Stepping in heartless ring alone handed him choices for
invisible traces and not time to spare,

Non-responsiveness to her attempted communication
stamped her as a solid simplified revolving door,

Motioning arms in direction of entwinement demanded the
chase in field for existence no more.

Scented Aroma Therapy

ଇଇଇ

Satisfied frame lays exhausted while eyes focus still and
mind revamps towards last night,

The touch positioned altering cognitive functions
in cognition reserving her on airline's flight,

Possessing therapeutic potential within his distinctive
smell lingered throughout silky sheets,

Subtle redolence trail of Bulgari Black cologne with body's
chemistry in senses enduringly meets,

Invisible suited alluring condition calmed the nerve like
geranium and reddened all her stress,

Visionary lifts towards unoccupied space above one's
anxiety non-confinement implying impress,

Immunity's response to inclining fragrant became her
alternative medicine for temporary cure,

If he solely meant as a valuable intermediate calculation
the imprinting will be transparently pure,

Until dominos fall into formation willingness entwinement
is the temporary presence sent,

While captivation resides in one midst of his scented
aroma therapy that's invitingly lent.

Love's Non-Residing Trace

ฮฮฮ

Minute of the hand patiently devoting her life
searching carefully to find,

Lonely tears fell onto moistened skin never cautioning eyes
towards going blind,

Arousing astonishment from deep within questions
his presence of being here,

Attempting persuasion in cognizance condition
that nobody supposed to be near—

Utmost love knocked at her eternity's residence
becoming mere optical illusion,

Provisions made for broken hearted security keys locked
towards her conclusion,

Closing portion of discoursed issue bonded
permitting entrance for the last time;

Quality duration spreads scorned wings at heart's
loneliness hollowed rhyme,

Circular sequential motion for advancement revolved
through staged exigency,

Confession by denial demanded her true emotions
towards life's aiding urgency,

Only his acknowledgeable perceptions
rehearsed her love's non-residing trace,

Inviting all that's consumed inside of him with an
open-armed soothing embrace.

Understanding a Woman's Heart

෧෧෧

Visualizing generosity within her inward spirit
by deleting words becoming consumed intimidation,

Never taken selfishly for granted one's scars instilment
from raised hand of a past elimination,

Realizing her becoming indifference reflecting natural
endurance towards growth's stages,

Valuing mind and body with one's soul reached pinnacles
cored essence through multiple pages,

Sharing compatibility's lane of interest uniquely defined
involvements path towards respect,

Issuing quality time without shifting gear's level towards
quantity's single most impure neglect,

Progressing patience entwinement of one's importance
with devotion to her God-sent kids,

Never feeling as if she's entering barrier gates from
amongst any deception or taken bids,

Concealed weapon for trust with loyalty allowed him
to sustain all her enduring painful scars,

His self-righteous and pure virtue had validated singular
stand suited entirely up to pars,

Medal of valor in man understanding a woman's heart
transformed her focus from afar,

Lowering on bended knee, vowing within entirety
positioning her heart above a floating star,

By the hand he takes grasp of fearful soul towards visual
sense allowing all transparently clear,

Placing a halt towards issuing within his completeness
sincerity's love and terminating her fear.

The Moonlight Path

පපප

*B*ristling winds settle the touch with tenderness
gently upon silky smooth rounding face,

Darkening shadows of surrounding atmosphere consulates
her presence of silencing place,

Weary structured frame staggers frontage forward view
refusing subsistence trials in defeat,

Downward rain of falling tears stream as blinding eyes
lower toward sand beneath her feet,

Stars hung in relaxing skies forming trails of footprints
sending messages for one's concentration,

Her walk slowly ascends into bareness glide while quiet
moment soaks inward deep penetration,

Mind is crowded with thoughts of clueless undeserved
misunderstanding for imprisonments stand,

Heart bleeds the longing sweet lustful softening kiss
as he lies upon his muscular land,

True alluring essence consumed amongst captive image
inhaled boundaries to rarely exceed,

Extending mental sort of mortal man destitute for
crowning deprives her arousing need,

Implying clear decision by drowning life in the moonlight
path decreased one's inflexible ride,

For she places all her tearful sorrows to drift swiftly
among collaboration's rhythmic tide.

Separate

୧୧୧

*H*eart matured by natural coursed advancement from
her injurious effective momentary pay,

Opinioned perplexing entanglement unit disclosed
utterance characteristics to even say,

She executed household technician duties as he invisibly
departed the entire calming night,

Once interception deluded his habitual style calculations
harmonized their battling fight,

Observing exertion of energy beyond lining from his
assured discreet telephone call,

Translucent capability comprehends this abiding man
transforming her residing life's downfall,

Awaiting his resting ground she summoned police
strongly stressing endurance of no more,

Existence has arrived for us to separate,
so don't ever attempt in kicking down my locked door,

Clueless implication questioned one towards configuration
applied corruptively in me,

Terminating travel's path of denying emotion refusing his
mere presence to ever again see.

Sentiments from The Heart

The Extraordinary Eagle

@

In Loving Memory of

Keithon Dontae Scott aka "Booh"

2/24/1990 - 11/22/1997

As the eagle sits with piercing eye,

Watching all as we go by,

Impacting in hearts his power of strength,

He won't rest until time had its length,

Why does he look at us without any fear?

It's the Lord's call he know is near,

Wondering why he always standing so tall,

The love one eagle has is for us all.

We never know when his time will ever end,

Just keep in heart the memories he spend,

Now stretch your neck and spread your wings,

For the Father's voice in your ears do so rings.

Soar through the air with no more worries,

For the impact of you have left many stories,

The day will rise and the night will go on,

But my dear eagle, in my heart you're never gone.

Always in My Heart

Woman of Devotion

ରେରେ

She stood firm feet pressed solid to ground,

Breaking bread to lost souls lurking all around,

Spreading God's word to visual deafening ear,

Praises of her song rings from afar and near,

Tambourine vibrates in dance as she joyfully shouts,

Leaving crowds clueless to what her jamboree was about,

Faith with patience in me she poured her entire life,

Maintaining on bending knee through each passing strife,

Gifted hands carefully stitched clothing
of one's masterpiece,

Piercing eyes focused sharply on each delicate lined crease,

Always awakening to aid my tearful late call,

Quickly screaming out in prayer pleading "Lord,
don't let her fall."

The heart she instilled inside as one woman
and devoted mother,

Unconditioned from her love truly
comparison is of no other,

So as I slowly close my eyes to deeply inhale
counting to seven,

Big Momma, remember my love for you always
while dancing around in heaven.

Your Granddaughter, Spicee Gray

Imprinted Melodies

ଥଥଥ

Uncle's love is unconditional for his niece,

Memories stored are a priceless unforgettable piece,

She looked at him with marbled glow in eyes,

As he contemplates on her maturity towards due time flies,

Remembering his niece smiling at arms' length glance,

While he played guitar in yard as her daddy dance,

She steps into now a grown woman's shoes,

Imprints of his face and her love, she will never lose,

In her heart he is truly missed,

For the card he sent she gently kissed,

Holding the masterpiece from her uncle to her chest,

Thinking in mind, "Uncle Squeaky, you are still the best."

If anything you get out of this heartfelt letter,

As your niece, my love don't diminish, it gets better!

With love, your niece

Wings of Merit

Rest In Peace

Our Sweet Mrs. Garza

૭૭૭

In life's choices, she mapped out each goal,

Her words of wisdom fulfilled one's soul,

She walked with grace, brightening every mile,

Imprinting her beauty and comforting portrait smile,

Her voice was sweet music to deafening ears,

Laughter echoed, erasing all depressing fears,

Heart's strength broke her numerous falls,

No matter how loud lightning storms call,

She lays in sand, gently closing her eyes,

Waves of water swiftly flow as time briskly flies,

Unknown presence calmly kneel to her side,

Softly whispering tears no longer have to hide,

Take my hand I'll guide you safely home,

Free from worries to have peace and joyfully roam;

Opening her eyes she began to stand,

Without hesitation, stretched out her hand,

Noticing her walk transformed into ascending merit,

As wings extended more valuable than diamond's carat,

Memories she engraved will continue to linger long,

Instilled wisdom remembered in the melody of a song,

As co-worker and devoted friend to everyone's heart,

Our memories with love for you will never part.

The Love Letter

In Loving Memory of my Grandmother,

Sister Lucille Mildred Williams
aka "Big Momma"

During troubling trials time you never denied your
Father's heavenly name,

Through the extensive heartaches in Him
you faithfully remained the same,

Boldly crossing over threshold tightly grasping
God's given worded sword,

Firmly standing still on solid ground fearlessly cutting
the extension cord,

Proudly serving singular reaping purpose against entirety
of distorted crowd,

Merely shouting His name so that surrounding souls
clearly heard you out loud,

Passerby's lurked with assumption baring opinioned
thoughts to misunderstand,

Your true call in position for Christ represented drums
within the roaring band,

Composure of me lingers long loving you
like any concealed debts of my heart,

All one devotedly instilled from wisdom's lock will never be
invitingly torn apart,

Remembrance remain so profoundly silent when you
positioned on bended knee,

Missing your bonding consolation while understanding
exhausted spirit's flee,

All memories extended with inviting wings soaring
towards light peering above,

Acknowledging peaceful comprehension like purity
of the signified white dove,

Pulsating motion to inhale and exhale counting
limitations towards number ten,

Granted dear Big Momma His arms spread wide
and you positively made it in,

So trust my painful tears are no longer towards sorrow
or endearments lost,

I am sincerely at ease knowing you're happily residing
within valuable cost,

Honestly if anything at all, my cheek towards greeting
I wholeheartedly miss,

Depositing tender sweet love expressed
in a grandmother's memorable kiss,

In closing of this last love letter I invisibly send through
pillowed Heavenly skies,

Keeping cognizant the love for you as tears fall downward
from my grieving eyes,

Sincerely and always, your granddaughter is stumping
instilments far from home,

P.S. Thank you for forty-two years upholding one in
prayers and unconditionally loving me...Shalom.

Closing

Thank you for taking the time to sit back and escape into the first book of poetry from words hidden within the depths of my heart. Allow me to personally introduce my upcoming autobiography, *The Hardened Heart*. This book is the essential ingredient that my poetry is derived from, and has given me the strength to overcome many obstacles in life's traveling trials.

I owe all to my Heavenly Father for providing me the wisdom towards the many years of writing this book in order to encourage and inspire many through my story. Take a deep breath, for you have experienced the enjoyment of sweet music through poetry which serves as a prequel to *The Hardened Heart*. Trust that once you have entered into my world of experiences and victory, you will be able to say, "This chain can be broken." Until then, farewell and I will meet you again upon the completion of my subsequent inscription. God bless you all and keep me in your prayer as I will do the same in return.

Love,

Spicee

About Spicee Gray

Spicee is a strong, independent single mother who fought to overcome emotional scars of abuse at the hands of those she felt would love her for the woman she's become. Abuse to her is not just physical, but also verbal and mental, which traumatizes anyone and gives the same effect. Spicee escaped from thirteen years of marriage to her ex-husband and another seven years with her youngest child's dad. In both relationships, she experienced traumatizing abuse which kept her from knowing the true meaning of love.

The one day came where she finally allowed herself to break walls and open her heart towards both loving and being loved, but surprisingly she came to the fork in the road, resulting in her being in love all by herself once again.

Trust that no one knew, not even Spicee herself, that she possessed— through the scars gained from storms in her life— the one key to acquire strength to fight fear and to stop hiding behind walls of control.

Will she ever find her true prince that will take her by the hand and show her what it means to be protected, comforted, and most of all cared for?

Only one place will tell: *The Hardened Heart*, a book of non-fiction written by Spicee herself.

Help support breaking the chain of abuse:

If you are a victim of abuse or know of someone that needs help, contact Family Violence Prevention Services, Inc. at www.FVPS.ORG or 210-733-3880.

Connect with Spicee or share your feedback on:

Amazon.com

Goodreads.com

 @SpiceeGray   /TheUnspokenHeart

THANK YOU FOR YOUR SUPPORT!

Purposely Created
PUBLISHING GROUP

YOUR WRITING IS A *Sacred* GIFT.

Your Words are more than an unbound manuscript waiting to be released into the world. It's a soon-to-be executed *divine assignment,* which can only be delivered by you.

The way it looks, feels and impacts is a direct extension of who you were **CREATED TO BE + DESIRE TO BECOME** #TheGreatest

It's Time to Unleash Your Manuscript!

Are you ready? #PublishYourGift

www.PurposelyCreatedPG.com

CONNECT WITH US!
(866) 674-3340
Hello@PurposelyCreatedPG.com
Facebook :: Twitter @PublishYourGift

To Avery

Thank you for supporting freaking the chain of Abuse.

Love.

Spicee '70

"The Unspoken Heart"
~Spicee '70~